NOCTIVAGATIONS

Noctivagations

Geraldine Monk

To Ann
With thanks

Geraldine Monk
2001

WEST HOUSE BOOKS – 2001

Published by
West House Books, 40 Crescent Road
Nether Edge, Sheffield S7 1HN

Distributed in USA by
SPD, 1341 Seventh Street
Berkeley CA 94710 – 1409

Copyright © Geraldine Monk 2001

Typeset in Bodoni
at Conversions Unlimited, Manchester
in collaboration with
Five Seasons Press, Hereford
and printed on Five Seasons
one hundred per cent recycled book paper
by Biddles Ltd, Guildford

ISBN 0 9531509 9 2

For Sam & Szilvia

Contents

THE

TRANSPARENT ONES

The Gathering

*(High noon. Mid Summer. Terrace. Round table. High
Peaks in the distance. Round robin of low sleepless talk.
The Transparent Ones)*

And in coming over it overcame. Shad. But blue. But.
But brilliant. Waterskin in Landlock. Shad-skein.
Highblownnoon encircled terminal.
Strangesobs. Cottonsoft blood. Pink. Candyfloss.
Balmfloat of stretched perception
Caught on. Celestial snag. Meteorite.
Nearer and nee. O. Orbiting. O Obit.
Catch us black inside.
'Cut us w'all bleed, w'all black inside'
Burnt sugar crystals. Brulée.
Sugarcrab.
Starspangled metastasis.
Ai! Comets come Acrashing.
AssssshhhhHHHhhhush . . .

Mood heightens. Speech plays tig.
Anticlockwise. Cockles tail. Wise. Ululations.
Moodblight. Moonlike drench of cloudcover.
Spirits crowd closer.
Branded collaborators.
The circle grews.
You (you) You (you) You (you)
Cellcreps.
Ringa.

AMOEBIC ENGULFING CLOSENESS

In a wide clean language turquoise is
uncomfortable.
It wafts from the Peaks with a gabbling of
green
and slippery mauve.

Around the table an odd coloured speech.
The one who twitters with
sprouting wings is not a
bird.
So sweet. So stop.
So weep. So weep
                with me
                    all of you.

Across Your Dreams in Pale Battalions Go

Rebel-woman outlaw-wise
halts me by that footfall.
Is gloom after all a
shade of hand
outstretched in
stargatherings?

*M recites
a memory*

Heap me over
this tremend love-
strange.
Piteous.
Futile thing!

*Pauses . . .
Roams . . .
Continues . . .*

From dank thoughts
that dangle
from the sighful
branchlets of
my mind.
Such is : what is to be?

*Reflected in
the mirror
she reflects:*

What's the big idea?
Lip to lip metwine wit
you in wind-walled palace
quaffing   quaffing.
The taintless chalice
is not above suspicion.
Lucent-weeping
glooming-robes
room-globing
purpureal
daysprinkt with
sad magic dust

A turn of
face she reads
the childs
Persephone

        Struct iz whip
        earthsplit down
        and downly in
        very-cold he
        carried

M shivers.
Shifts unease.

        flowers wept
        crops stopt
        leaves turned
        raged-red
        and shed
        everything
        shed

In the deep
midwinter

        Still life.
        Mourning.
        Snow.
        Six glacial
        pomegranate
        setting sun
        seeds.

Bluehound

'nix y'am no-am man-nor-beast save once I sate
life's banquet feast-y-eating my own little words—
stealing their happy away'   J.T.

But where
are we going?
And what is
it all about?

Going
we are where
about all it is

Does it really
matter
where's
my friend?

Matter really it does
friend my-my
trying to grasp your wagging
tale cart-wheeling away
big-hearted thinks
force ten laughs
beltering through
philosophical doors taking
flying
Looby Loo's
at the ill wind.

It is time
to go now?

Haul away the
anchor.
Your imminent
Alien State awaits your
sailing,
Pet, wipe your eyes
at the
coming of your
dazzling
ufo
afterlifeboat

So life's
like that?

       Like an ilk love on a gnarled
       hand *in* glove *in* tongue *in*
       cheek *in* stitch *in* time does
       its doing with
       your natter-flack
       questions creating
       ineffable Q systems &
       split infinities

And that is
that?

       Pup-a-luv —
       that is that

Then paste this question mark to the centre of the sun

Cliff Hanger

In the midst
came the end

Well there you go . . .
dropped off your perch
quiet as a mohair scarf . . .
just like your best dream
dreamt of . . .

Leaving me

me-all   a-drift
all-in a day's work
with a mouth full
of unsaids so I'll
have my sayso now

With glitches
& gremlins

The computer scanner
drew a blank
so no o.k.
you'll not make it
to my birthday
though we both knew
you wouldn't go
to the bitter ends of
your ancestral dig
into colourful
meaning
deeply
shady crooks
and songbirds
hooking
more than
even we
bargained
for.

convergence
of spookilies

My do at
Eckington Hall
fell through a stone
's throw from
Renishaw
's dragon flies spell
trancing aerial
hieroglyphs
in-non-rhyming
couplets.

Japanese
fancy-fish tail
us humans to the sharp
corners of geometric
ponds blowing
kisses of life
poised –

Scaling
the heights

So here is the
where the winter list
and shiver of Christmas
trees await their moment
where your old
man's old man's
beard & fiddle
scaled
carousal singing
stately gates
rocking and
shocking the
maids and ever
so young Lady
Sitwell with
child-wild
Plantagenet
poet.

Keltic Twilight

Swanz

Tin throated
keltic sotto voce
soothing grubber pants
o drizzlings.
Impy-eyed & turned up
lipping 't-poep-sa-nutter'
Papa Dub.

Snakerz

'Apostasy'
you hizzles
warmly Romewards
'Apostasy!'
with no remorse
enstrangling holythrone
enshrined
Joh-Pau
rocks
his serpent.   *Rock.*
We're talking holy *see.*
See you lisps the obscene
usurps

*The oracle
shakethz*

'I saw the aurora in '38'
(she said we would)
highlarks & jinxloons
beaking awesome through the
bannering ore-glow diagonal
t'wards the second W.W.
Alpha es et O.

*Tales of
scary
miracles*

Three children of Fatima
all told were asked
by her white-robed self
in the whiter heat of day
'are you ready to suffer'
And lo! The Portuguese
field of vision became a
landing strip the
size and bustle of
Heathrow.

Truncheoned candles ignite
both ends the prophecies
of brightday runaway minds.
Religious tack is truly cruel
and the crude sun on its knees
remains unmoved. Unblooded

we abs-orbit with Abdul.
Be mused. Thinking on
accuracies of Old Mother
Shipton.

The oracle
ascends

'APOSTASY'
liplix again
with hands down
eyes
winnin-grin
full of guinness
brimmingly
you passes on
your borrowed
flowers
flit
in two my
giggly
palms

Then One Morning

She points her
missy
ring-ripped
no-finger

    'For you.' 'For me?' 'For you.'
    'Really?' 'Rely upon me.
    Living alone in a back-flat.
    Companies of g-howls an g-hosts
    through the nesh nights of aloneness
    I noticed you. For you. Really.'

I read her
words to me
she makes a
covenant

    I will re-yern as a snowflake.
    Be-back as a solitary drop
    in a flurry.
    I will land on the outermost
    tip of a
    nose-end and tickle.
    Trickle & treat
    to evaporate with
    out pain
    or maybe-be the
    one flake that
    breaks the bough
    off-of a certain
    tree.

She seers
my unspoke
love

    Kittywakes whirling.
    'Marry him'
    she yellows at my
    goodbye back
    turned
    eyewhites gone daffodil
    sheshines and
    hurls her voice ceilingward.
    Upperstraight.
    See through.
    Oracular.
    !Do it!   *Exitstage Flowerless Left*

The Unspeakable Softness of Flesh

Skin Panics.
even our words are ridd~~led.
Sense disappears at every touch.
Ideas dissolve before formulation
(uncertainties sneak round corners)

Aqueous morphine alcohol & fear
confuse all the terminals.
Messages splinter
inter
mutant Gethsemanes of agony.

Betrayal is sexual ~~
illusory beauty exquisite.
Hands join in supplication
hands spread flesh spread
death parted lips do
do drip dreadfully
'your future's all used up'
she husks to the ever swelling strain
of the Pianola spook.

In the grip of rising panic
we watch the solitary unleaf furl ~~
There are moments of relief
in every fiction

so go get the lilies . . .
your doppelganger just rode into town
sprouting wings
is not a
bird.
So sweet. So stop.
So weep. So weep
            with me
                all of you.

TRILOGY

La Tormenta

(With plundering from The Tempest)

Heat that Feb ice. Spell melt.
T'wild frozen waters in that
ittered sky pelt downd
sunless pitch
jagged — it pricks the
soft cheeky brains. Afeard minds.

S'long Inglaterra. S'long Orchard Square.
Us runaway names listing wreckerlessly
t'be cast stoneyed taxiing down
the airy all ways of eternity.

Upslung at last orgasmic gasp
hook off nerves
stripped bare eyes
leaking resinous pollen.
Crying:
What! Must our mouths be cold?

(you are young you said
you must enjoy your
self who died beyond the
nine lives
of cats)

Sprit guide riding high.   Mischef meker.

Not half-drunk enough. Not half-love.
Even when an hourish later
paprika earth hit us at half-slant
dazzling unexpect of spice
heating hot
appalling hungers for
everything but food.

Cravedaze. Not half.
Half-nod cut. Enough.
Rubbed crimpt eyelids
seez duty freez vanish.
Who put wild water in this roar?

An unsettled fancy is upon us.
An unwrit score rewrit.
'Fasten your seat belts' says Bette,
at the foot of the bumpy stair.

With flickt wrist
t'heavens
ope'd.

Sonic bullroarers
neckstretchers
stampeders on the wing
shaking living daylights
oust our dreading bones.

Toss't dice.   Yinegar.

Fly blowed.   Hoisted.
D Day One.   Godlost.
We split we spit farewell!

(tricksy spirits were abroad)

Down
and slumped in
sting of godglitz
weighted with static
collective
thankingyee sighs
tongue tips kiss
grit and tracery of dog
shit soft staining drinks
stick-a-lips — cling film — clung
filigree of dead skin
glitter dust fag ash
cheek to check a
signature of some body's blood
drip-written on pave stones.

Foreign forest floor.
           terror terra firma
                 WONDEROUS HEAVY.

Landlocked

In this cloud-capped city
some will lose fear of
violent fragrance and all things gold
by accident most strange in
flamed amazement: sometimes we'd divide
and burn in many places.
Bars. Backstreet grooves. Esquinas.
Lying plazas. Round squares
Rare wantings. Melancholy daemons.

Duende's all the raging.

Crike in the open-mouthed night
no(t)ches glass gem
bled red gaps I lost one rapid
drift along the length of my body
it dripped from my ring
shoosh . . . shoosh . . . shoosh
slow
as
rose
hip
syrup.

Red bleddings

teeth sink in
Toledo
Chinchón
chin´chin chin´chin chin´ch´
in
deeply seedy bikers
bar the music of
pomegranates
anchovies
well oiled fish
slivers.

We cannot believe
our very-eyes oh yes our
very-eyes we cannot believe
Sopa Goyesca La quinta
creps del sordo
vegetal in season
and what we ask has
Tarta comtessa
got in store
topped only
by an earthenware owl.

Gauze-flutter of curtains
spook the white room dumb
blanca deep dancing
these bangled wings and
rusty swords in the

                              dead of corridors

such stuff as dreams are made of . . .
rabid sadtoned arabesques . . .
hip sways . . .
death riffs . . .
brave new heart-beats

                    chin´chin chin´chin chin´chin
                        chin´chin chin´chin chin
                            chin´chin chin´chin
                                chin´chin chin
                                    chin´chin
                                        chin
                                        ch

Prague Spring

When the Russians rolled in I
was selling papers to
agents and
Alexander Dubček
became a name to pronounce

Broadsides not quite the length of Wenceslas
Square dripped tanks off the edges anon
my sixteenth birthday
I catched the
grainy grey images
of a-dying people
and put them in my pocket
the way you do with falling stars

> **In a Prague spring of thirty years later**
> I stumbled off the beaten track
> narrowly not killed on Petřin
> hill the night they burnt witches over
> the river for
> being women and missing
> the mirror maze totally

> To land was not to fly but scamper and
> burrow through the undergrowth trying
> to find the after-curfew lights and
> fast food is sure as sure a
> cruel oxymoron to the lost
> longing soul and hungry

Over the river there is
always the other side of the river where
Princess Libuše gathers a single mushroom
sighing heavy with visions:
the god warriors will come a-godding
a-good king will bury his hatchet
in the holy rood
Vitus will fling
and five days after Agnes
is sainted
the velvet revolution   begins

Darkly clever jokes fill darker
pubs at weedle-ends glacé cherryful eyes
stain-cults of fine bohemian isinglass
intensely lumes from nooks
older than digged up roman teeth.
— *it wasn't a million years ago miners used fishskins*
for light in tin mines in-ingland —
but if Chamberlain sold them down
the river
a more beautiful
river is
hard to be sold down

Down the cellar the dregs still
left: the overstayed
falling
dreamily with love:
two soft speaking men
knives and bright forks
thick blackbent tablesunder
stiffstarch whitestuff
and us with us under
flamewick spell

From three bears to
white ox in a matter of
centuries the floor
length apron opened
and underhanded the
samizdat menu:
'Giant Mountain cabbage soup'
'Game from our Meads and Copses'

With squat poppy΄out eyes the
medieval denim-clad sword swallower
unswallowed then rammed two six inch
nails up his nostrils for dessert putting
one off our pudding and one
off our dumplings but neither off our
BECHEROVKA which kicks
stomach pit spreading
molten with herby-ore
ace primer for the
land of lurid fairytales

(Golem Watch)

What is Golem?

Artificial-man made-clay
Servant-savant
Key fig o magikyl Praha
un
finisht
coarse
lopt

How did Golem look like?

Drest asa shammes
mythical mudman
tall puft features
hal-met-like hair-heavy
buskin shoes
jacket pressed parchment
    like a jazerant
        like armour padded cotton hardened
           in salt water astec warriors
                wore
                war-h

How does one make a Golem?

One must purify oneself then
one forms a pup
        pet from vir
           gin earth and
walks it
    in a cir
        cle while
    re
      citing
the letters of the tet
        ra
        gram
IN FOUR HUNDRED AND SIX (SIC)
PER
MUTATIONS

How make Golem move?

One writes the word EMIT
                    (truth)
sharp on its forehed *(sic)*
or places the SHEM in his mouth

How does one the Golem destroy?

By walking it in a circle in the op
po direction while reciting alpha
bet backwards as a curseplaying close
attentions to the number of turns
the combinations of
lettersand
the way one walks

and the way one walks
              one walks

(The Last Day)

On the way to **Kutná Hora**
we met a lonely man
a loney man we met there
he was a **Russ´i´an**

      On taking of his photo
      our fate snapped in his hands
      disappearing out the blue
      blaze offa the earth face
      he stole our lacy plague-bothered bones

            Oh unseen ossuary built on the back
            of a half blind monk
            30,000 bodies ram-racked
            and shackled in a death dance
            of monstrances urns and chandeliers

                  Our last chance day
                  fractured with your flight &
                  splinter
                  growing eye-sockets
                  wide as saucer dogs
                  filling up wi-watery question
                  marks drip
                  Oh where Oh where did our Russ´i´an gone?

                        In the **Hotel Europa** life goes
                        with a slowhand peeling
                        paints seen betterdays
                        worsen
                        the $\mathbb{C}$o^{l}aMac$A$me^{r}ic$_{a}$n^{a} brays
                        its ways across the oblong
                        squaring
                        he-haw yea-haa aw gaud
                            y
                            cheap perfume bottles
                            glister with
                            peacocks and
                            petals
                            fall backwards on the
                          blackened
                          statues
                          hulked histories
                        volute in their
                        see-through
                      STONE-LODESTAR

Prelude V

The moment the pin pricked Venice
the Bridge of Sighs
                              answered
number one
                    across
the quick
Gondolier
                    cascaded
down the cryptic
Rialto
          drew
first blood
on University
                    Challenge Don't
Look Now
               peered
out the Tee Voo
through morning mists
and western portentous
voodoo
blinds shuttered sight
seeing
cross connections
snaking round our anklets
for snake forms also part of
everything
in   this
      s
   link
      y

I stood in Sheffield on the Building Sites
A navvy and a nutter on each hand
Part actors rising from their rubbled souls
Italiano-tyke bellowed without
end Or elegance Or diphthong
BonJorno BonJorno MoltoBeLLA
bellowed with conspiratorial glee
a noise-filled pause from
neo-classical concrete.
Breeze-blocked.

Swoop in two Js
and don't say
'Venice is rubbishy'
as Claude slayed Rome
but solely praised only
fish market:
of a city built in staggering
beauty on bracken
the fish must have been
unearthily spectacular

We fly on Halloween
nocturnal revel
                    destinies
borne down by evidences
over the Alps half
                    a
year to the
                    day

Walpurgisnacht
unwittingly our wedding
eve driven
passion
for
lilies
snow whitened
witch sab
mountains

Faustus
in whim for wheeze
announces
sensation creation in Venice
courtesy of devil-aid
lifted sheer from
Piazza to Pointless
on Satan's stickle back
haunches —

but brutto-face lets him fall
        a   a
      r   r
        i   i
          a   a
he Faustus hee
nearly gives
up his ghast

'When people propitiated their gods
they stereotyped the limits of their minds'

All in a flitter
dwarf clib-clobs the
calles
hoofin
initsitsybitty
P.V.C. redderhooded
rainmares
dousing the soothsayers
with convulsions and
blindeyed
doubters

e mio marito non can swim
floats in cyberspace
with ease without life
belt wrapped
around
where my arms
wrap around —
physical to abstraction

Whilst Byron stood
number 1
              across
the 4th canto
I randomly opened the page:
'to separate contemplation'
it stops me in my flow of
webbings against the naggering backdrip
of monomaniacal rains and flu

— I need oil´skin — nurofen —
we'll all Autumn '98 need
well-connected toes like
mother's born before
they cut them. Cut them?

Anti-amphibian disformists!

No sooner gone than back flips
a postcard from Zennor
and reckons once
                across
a time
a mermaid married and
married to atone to a
sweet tone of +cultural divides
and separate contemplation

So Mary born before my time —
as mothers tend to be —
uncut-aquatic water-babe
wimmerswims upstream > > > >
from Lido to Piazzale Roma
beating Byron flappers down.
But we just KoKo'd jumped the
Vaporetto
feet dry 'n' cosy down its
Grand
S
Kaly
S
pinebone

Hit one more nail
in the kitch wall
to hang suspension~~~~
the hand that sent Zennor
daubed Adriatic reds
and oily sets of
sun bloods and oranges
and even as it dries

cool Canaletto comes to York
undaunted by its 'Micklegate Run'
notorious
he stashes the entire
Grand Canal under his
carnival cloak

quivering angelica in aspic

— still falls the rain
on England &
Wales
turns to rivers and ruins and
each house will
build a shipshape
makeshift gondola
and it will cost us
all nothing at all
to sail to Clapham Common
or Wherever
and why go to Venice
when Venice comes to us
at the drop of its name
in a ceaseless drip . . .

SONGINGS

& STRANGERLINGS

Songings

Stoop rich fruit through nothingness
caress and be a steeper bliss.
Neon slips the storm.
Seizure of light.
Some fear to lose the day.
The lioness maymove
o'er her prey.

Carved in the heart
a rusting ring-
serpent split
eternity.
Your image turns to
arctic flakes
such craving
burnt the trusty tree.

Deepest abyss.
A will-o'-the-wisp
rock heavily my mind.
Sea-lured river-wracked.
Hovering night
drench calmly
the harm-quake
drench calmly the
quake.

*

Be still
unresting limbs
frantic as birdsong.
Come now shades
a-lingering sleep
wallowin
creature me.
No words to strangely
work the heart.

Take love easy
bid grow deep-feather-down.
Ocean rumours favour with a-flow
no sadness on me
weepingo.
In the land of strangers be
lost be lost
in me.

How long
have we known
songs grow not
on trees — longer than
longings
may spring
unrestrained
sing yeah — sing nay
sing-sigh.

Breakers rave her
dis tresses
round
scattered ruins
ruined
sleight of banished
hand throwing hearts
the card . . . the knave
of darts . . . darts . . .

Air this strain
mug
lemon heave of ebon
mammatocumulus
westwarding westward
refrain
unhallowed sky
forests foraging
doom
raddle the core
raddle
refrain.

To bite this temperate fruit
sweet
sinned and purpled
with vigour.
Unmask the melody
locked and languishing
on the tip . . .
tongue the
soft-fell
pash.

Stay! Stay!
Jealous Season
proud with fame-
glorious conflagration
roaming constant
flocks of . . .
flocks of . . .
etherise.
Stay! Stay!

Arctic wings bring
exquisite gloss.
Holy-l-ice
fast-gathering
phantoms
land
on hill
on brow
on temples.

Peach-glad tree tips
night notes throated
steep
fleeting
continual
enwrap feet
with angel-high-wires
mandrake cumber
world
turn-turtle.

Be still my
float-a-bout
soul
until the
hasting hurt greets daffo
days a-parts the
gold embroidered gorgeously
unstained.

Setting bird
la-light on ultra
woodland
violets
fabulous
crystalline
lining
dimples weary
winter
captive wilt
not.

Roman Rumourals

I

Lest heat flash from eyes
surge burst the breast
as if from grape
bear my sour words
find the names!

II

After dressing in reddish robes
plucked green slippers fresh from a bag
four gorgeously decorated feet
filled with admiration
moved toe-wards civil war

III

My eyes his figure
towards him turned
crossed out sight
undone my thought
hallowed spot knot

IV

Degrees overcome one groan
sorrow wet lumps of frankincense
lack a-grave design
light limbs light limbs
win me death

V

Central space totters forth
all bare and open
a nameless trunk
a drunkless head
huddling like doves

VI

Raving past control so bright
that darkles end I hate
huge blocks unfixed
trembling as for life
markle me

VII

Herself the first
but far within
(bar no guard) crouching dirk
water surges in a heap
the long headlong voured

VIII

Force wins her footing
incrush curst
staining the hearth
hackered door reels
reels rush rushes

IX

New dread omen-locks
on outer ness sets dens
maw-maw
holy signs spill ugly
heads is knit

X

Sea we wend to
fl-flutter soul awayless
meat upon gold
come tell the tale
salt your seer mouth

XI

Wax-a-cold
bend the rowers wand
double deadly blood
super-posed
pre-modial

Strange Bud True

Despite ever increasing knowledge
remote stars remain remote.

*

Blood is thicker than but water is more
speaking volumes — the sentiment despite.

*

Thicker than the thin crust the outer
core hued and almost black schists.

*

Light-hype the holy-tides love.
In Merrie-Eng marigolds are summer brides.

*

She died no great outer beauty from eating
melons. Her tomb came to light.

*

Under the horses hooves a deep pit opened the
age of merry-goth-follies.

*

Then catalystic cow climbed the spiral staircase
and plunging down deathwards the pit closed.

*

And everybody knew the Vichy were beautiful skin-
masters of the deathwards double-cross.

*

Rotor-ship enthusiasts predicted Vichy water
thicker than blood would hit the fan.

*

Stabbed in the heart. An amazing background.
Solitary clue. Fan. Faked body theory.

*

With traces of human ghosts on her solitary
hands her lover's dagger children stibbed.

*

The University prepared Earth's early atmosphere.
Bade power. Brit petroleum. Stibbed lightning. Brisk.

*

Men pursued embroidery. Women went to sea-wars.
Power of facts. Fishy. Strange unravelling of non-history.

*

The Turk unravelling Russian meant nothing to Vienna.
Suspended by threads the chess bored man applied heat.

*

Spain: heat of agony and incident. Faces on kitchen floor.
Spectral eyes could not be scrubbed: wider and wider not out.

*

Behind frosted glass. Obscure references. Cutting bread.
Reconstructing past past. Scrubbed route without words.

*

The Doomwatch Dragons was not a tea urn. Or rock ruck.
When a ground shock occurred a reconstructing reconstructing.

Fairy Tales From Nether Edge

Tinder Talk

'Well I must sleep outside under this stormy visit'
The dry skin creaked aloud.
'Oh I shall not be afraid. What will look like will look.'

Little Snow Bones

When evening came all over
it came all over
depleted wooden soldiers
fell heavier held
uranium as
stiff and immovable as
no one
upon a
no leg.

The Wishing Thief

Now you must not imagine that there is nothing.
Our rooms with fishes are bolder than swallows
and all flaws and little bubbles inside articles
are not defects
for the flowers of the Yorkshire floods are scentless.

Clever Little Ragamuffins

Heaven with all its stars was above them
and the town so impatient.
If they glue his back back together and put
the first word that they heard in this world
exquisitely and absolutely
back
just so
stars was above them.

The Ugly Strange Beauty

When she returned she had a thousand things to
relate: many an evening would the five sisters rise
hand in splendour and exchanged heavy crowns for
flowers of the garden which were so much more
shook and thanking you for the granted preference.

The Pack of Sweet Porridge

All but exhausted and with great difficulty
keeping his round smile kindly
and upon him — for her.
There were many
things that she wished to hear to
control her sorrow at
not having
an immortal soul
ever after
the modern design.

The Poor Empty Briar Bottle

I will prepare for you a drink which you must
require in exchange
for my magic drink which you must
require I shall be a
sleep were asleep a sleep.
Lamps in the saloon must be extinguished.
Railtrack will move.

Sleeping Star-money

She would not go in for she could not speak.
Alas so mournfully she beckoned to him
over the wild waves in the wooded bay
where the holy temple stood.
Glancing at the sky she saw the dawning light
through the atmosphere perfumed with
delicious probation.

The Global Snow Queen

In the middles of the driven
palais frozzen midden lake
s'called t'cold mirror of reason
sit a working pair of hands
not forming the letters
to make E-T-E-R-N-I-T-Y
endless to take
the whole world.

A mean test
and riddance goody t(w)o:
A twin of splinters in
the eye 'n' heart wi-warmth.
A kiss away from meltdown.

She is not amused the
polar bears can now stand on their
own two hind paws exhibiting
themselves in
the oddest positions in
the whole world.

The . . .

Listen! When we arrive at the end we shall know.

DREAM DROVER

Dream Drover

don't grip the lip
    crossed arms breed a twisted
      see that tree
        believe you-me doing this
          is an undoing of dreamera
            and right on top of our love run!

        Lesson One is
        pure Peak scree
      slam on the anchors
      the one ditched on its
    lid among the 'eather and
    rabbit currents
brings a ring o rozzers in the wilder-ness

todaze of all the days
  to be not go rund the benz
    is all is axed
      blind alley lou-laa
        wilt not I prey or
          bolshie be in this life
            err agen ift keep me uptickt
            and lid-righted

            This: secs splitter to re-knit
          tighter as choker do
        away this hapless
      and hurted un-reel
      to get to the point
      Thee
    point is upon zoomzinzoomz
    oo-my down dread
  my absent sweet-swaying heart
  here is the here-now
 where the world drops awa
    y

It has always been . . .
it no-more always be . . .
a mind-drift shifted
this-a-way an that
as the crosswinds
blow-out stretches at a-glancing
and you needn't hold back
to see clearly ahead —
hey ho!

A'm doing this
A'm believing not
A'm doing dream time-big
As tra-laa partial star sashays
its hexy little bott
om down the mountill
be caught in the arms of Hathersage
withat Little-Bugger-
John snoring in
his ghost grave
scheming dreams
of young Liz
Taylor shimmying into
Bronte skin
!woah!

Outside operation hours
a surgeon over stitches
in double quick
a logjam of astral bodies
blow horns a la cors anglais
too-too impatients park + glide
theatrics glassin ceiling
an un-free-flowing
non-exceeding speed

(in a bedsit   two lovers   accidentally miss-a-kiss)

and it goes or it went
as if am-not
and the disembodied
. . . . voice-over gonging
gas-gas-gas

backer ups wego
for oration and light
facula fandang
go leaving sheep none the wiser
in their exquisite intactus
you Well Dressers
grub and gath anothers
seasons petal art
perdy pics
in dip elation I try arithmeticals . . .
how many foxhouses
must two come across
at differential
differents inlife
or some such

Re-entering the city
words shirk desired objects
by the bikers doz
flock off wingering —
pressing *pebbles* is not *bon mot*
and should be stimped un
only in emergence
and I cannot overmake
the sign
of the
X
to find my right
is not left
blinkin'
L

Godda gedda
witness
let me point out
(but twill avta be with my nose)
Ringinglow came
fastas papier confetti
yin may rain and wind flut
it fleet like a goer
gold is the colour
is the metal magicky
circuit
invisibly replete tied
bright with parallels

HIDDEN CITIES

Hidden Cities
(A tour)

Welcome all of you . . . involuntary ghosts of tomorrow
. . . scoring future imprints down the roads and junctions
of unmarked time . . . welcome to the imperceptible slice
between now and now . . . the progression of idle
nanoseconds.
Welcome to Manchester . . . Funchester . . . Gunchester
. . . Madchester . . .
Journey with me now and regain a return to where we
almost started . . . journey through the making of each
suspended sentence . . . spectral word . . . half breathed
comma . . . shifting metropolis . . . through these unofficial
urban arteries of time-ticking creatures . . . glossed out
histories . . . contrived artefacts . . . accidental spaces.

WHITWORTH STREET WEST

We start and shiver in this place of a once deep industrial valley swathed in pigs-wallow peoples-wallow kids-wallow deep in the flooding cellars of greedy disease. Famine now levelled with concrete guilt . . . palaces of fun. A past under our feet skewered with stations of unconsecrated crosses.

Looping the central containers of information, controlled culture, civic control: central library, art galleries, tourist info-bureaux, town hall concert halls, halls of illusion, delusion, doctored knowledge, half truths, half imaginings, other worlds. Obligatory bastions of external good taste hiding internal broodings, oblique questions, spider-runs, furry rodents. Civic pride beaming bright-eyed.

Defensive buildings, elegantly paranoid, massively assured, pompously benign. Facades honed and chiselled into full fisted hieroglyphs, curlicues, copulas . . . other loveable fripperies.

A magnificence built on the blood of slavery. Red raw cotton. Strange hanging fruit.

Scattered assortment of crawling monuments . . . stiff upper memorials . . . meeting places of minds and lovers . . . the massacred . . . the slayers of sense. Stylized in-sanity. In get it. Eh. In. Get.

Crack this heart open. Open like an egg. Open like a head and out oozes dross and speckled stardust, dates and data, rates for the right to live warmly, fates scrawled in still born words.

Crushed human nature lies bleeding in fragments all over the face of society. All over the pavements BLAST in the FULL LIGHT of our immaculate candelabras. Chandeliers.

ANCOATS

The city burst upon our minds at every repeating sudden . . . heaving
impressions illuminate the unrehearsed streets a wakening for
another night . . . see the bodies floatwalk . . . wigging the full bloods
and luminous skins . . .

So onwards to Ancoats to leave our ghost smeared down the Great
Old Artery. Down Redhill, Old Mill Street past the overstretched,
drained Old Hospital.

Even in the sickly dark flying birds are mouths: mouths flying birds.

Leaving this place of critical
hurt and psycho-catastrophe
this place where children roamed half
giddy with the noise and endless
motion sweeping between
machines of the most beautiful
contrivance spreading and wafting
between the teeth half giddy kissing
the shuttle and sucking
a cop through the eye of
a beautiful contrivance and so
says all the seven year old bodies
between teeth and kissing the shuttle
with gum disease spreading and
wafting and sucking a cop between
machines spreading soft dirty
yarns through white milk
teeth kissing the shuttle half giddy
sucking the yarn dirty
between the most beautiful
contrivance and now we
squeeze between machines and
secrete our own psycho-smears a
long this great grieving artery . . .

grieving . . . grieving . . . grieving . . . grieving . . . grieving . . . grieving

CHEETHAM HILL. STRANGEWAYS

Land of wholesalers
    warehouses
    hidden goods & useless goodies
    enrapt with dog-eared dayglopainted signs.
    Shouting pink. Hurting green. See-me red. Scalding black.
    Buy-me middle-men. Unnamed tradesters. Stairwells of no
    return
    overshadowed by the thickest walls. Slidey walls.
Strangeways walls
    deliciously curved. Even so it is a masculine building.
    A men-only building.
    Note the watchtower.
    Note inside: all turgid with pain stuff.
All grit. All prickles. All tiny broken up bits of crunch stuff.

The oscillatory disequilibrium of cells originates from external causes.
Microbe unicellular organisms acting by virtue of
their own radiation.
Their own aggression.
Invasive patterns excite.
Gnaw. Guttle. Engorge.

Under their prison beds gritty bits of dead skin quiverrrrrrrrrrrrr

DEANSGATE. URBAN HERITAGE PARK

Past the radiation of railways and rivers.
Cathedral radiations.
Infrastructural radiations.
Innumerable radiations.
Past past and evernow.

A meeting of colourscapes.
A meeting of patter and shapes.
To take away. To-go.
To feed arterial space with motion and redness.
Yes with bloodish things
Good citizens meeting in the halfway house of bloodish things meat
dreams in the interstate of awakeness and sleep the mutual invasion
shattering into unending multiples. Unending arches.

(Directions are lined with unbroken shops for a decent, he said, *and
cleanly,* he said, *external appearance,* he said, *suffice to conceal
from the eyes of wealthy men,* he said, *and women of strong
stomachs and weak nerves,* he said, *the misery and grime which
form the complement of their wealth,* he said, *this hypocritical
plan,* he said, *is more or less common to all GREAT cities,* he said)

Now sandwiched inbetween the odd pub, club and seedy
looking for some action
to wake the little creepy animals
in our tug-of-blood centre.

So need to speed past Urban Heritage Park, museums, preserved
dirt and over there chuck-flipping Granada Studios oh and yeah
National Ga-ga-gas Gallery it's a Gag?

These great constrainers.   Retainers of a subreal pretty-polly
pecked past. Let's get past. *Let's rip and pour the full brimming
piss-pots full of genuine piss-not . . .*

SALFORD QUAYS

Iron bridges scuttle & butt & fly off handles &
criss crossly & hump & arch & girded loins

as we cross into the old Wapentake space opens and shuts. Breathes.
Beats.   Moves as we move.   Space between brick and brick.
Shapechanging.   Gaping.   Yawning.   About to swallow.   Space
between hoardings. Horrors. Between railings. Wet city flowers.
Space beneath our feet. Between the floor and the road and the
sewers. Open. Drains. Now shut. Now ope. Space that weeps.
Contracts. Cramps. Space that seeps. Space veins. Arterial. Pale
drained spaces.   Breathe.   Beat.   Swallow.   B.eating   B.eating
B.eating B.eating B.eating B.eating B.eating B.eating B.eating B.eating
B.eating B.eating B.eating B.eating   B.eating B.eating B.eating B.eating B.eating B.eating
B.eating B.eating B.eating B.eating B.eating B.eating B.eating B.eating B.eating B.eating B.eating B.eating B.eating B.eating   B.eating B.eating B.eating   B.eating B.eating B.eating

HULME

Passing the septum.
The movable no-go territorial stamp stamp.
Unguest land of twitching lace.
Nervous curtains . . . chop off your gaze
(mop it up . . . . . . *mop it up*)

And some sort of door here and there opens. Un-opens.
Inch-opens . . . slit face . . . and another . . . unlit . . .
in the blood breathing shadows
(brood breeding shadows)
in the unlit imperceptible slice between now
and now and
face

future ghosts of the city

X-ing territorial membranes.   Unseenable.   Unguest terrors.
Hexing.   Unguessed traces.   Lodged fast.   Break in scape.

See those bodies floatwalk?
Wigging the full-bloods and luminous skins.
Stragglers and loveable fools —
soft and
jammy 'ard — as nails — hot foundry

And the floatwalkers dreamon by . . . daubed and blighted with
shadowcast with bright-light with nibble tease of neon
topas amber sulphur sodium ghastlygreen

'There ain't no government like no government.
Uz loonies. You scumbags.'

And the morning after the night before pavement after the happy
hour night before the day even started it turned sour and a fist
kisscurled into fright and like magic knuckles everywhere whiten-up
and the wide-boys leg it like fucking pelicans.

So what's new in the rearrangement of stomach contents and the ever
beating peristalsis eating.b eating.b eating.b eating.b eating.b eating.b
eating.b eating.b eating.b eating.b eating.b eating.b eating.b eating.b eating.b
eating.b eating.b eating.b eating.b eating.b eating.b eating.b eating.b eating.b eating.b eating.b eating.b eating.b eating.b eating.b eating.b

(Cities conspire to wreck the heart)

(UNLOCATED)

So all this past is come to pass and a body aches / in one place and
then another / body aches in another / place and a face / cracks and
creaks in time to / some emotion or another time / is faced and the
space is vacated / and another is filled with / a past and a body that
ached in / one place and then another body ached in another place
and a face cracks and / creaks in time to emotion / or another time
is / faced and the space is vacated and another is / filled with a past
is / come to pass and a body aches / in one place and then / another
body aches in one place / and then another / body aches in another
place and a face cracks and creaks / in time to some emotion or
another / time is faced and the space is vacated / and other time is
filled with / a past and a body cracks / and creaks in time / to some
emotion or another filled / with a past and a space ached in one
place and / then another space ached and filled with a face and other
and / another in time to vacate with emotion with another / is come
to pass this past is come to pass and a body aches in one place / and
/ another is filled / and / a space is vacated and a face cracks and
creaks in time to time to emotion in / one space to ache / then
another face is filled with a past / and another past is filled / and a
face is vacated and a body aches and cracks and aches and creaks
and cracks to / time to time to time is filled with vacated with filled
with vacated with space / with aching space / with aching emotional
place / so all this body so all this past so all this ache is come / to pass
and another and another is and another is and another and is and

TWO DRAMATICS

Manufractured Moon

(Subject: Fox barks)

Sat upright and owl-eyed for hours so thoughts got to pellets &
droppings of words but to longhand e-mail or fax foxes barking
trees weeping their sticky in the early hours flashing sodium tales in
the techno light show of all night club fang.

City animals on their eternal nocturnal party rounds. A fox is
burying meat pies in the pitch dark of a first division football feud.
Dive, dribble and chip in the centre. They will hunt and bray it
down the four lanes and dual carriageways of the ringing roads.
Wild life and night birds cluster round the heart of metropolitan
hip-hop-scotch. Farmer farmer may I cross your golden river . . .
game from the streets.

Dawn will finally break me into the land of nod and off I go like
yesterday a man got shot two streets away.
Come up and see
me sometime.
Getha

(Subject: Hungered and Loafing)

Fresh air in my city lights. I breath soft sofas of joy. I cross off the
calendar days. I cross them backwards. They meet the ones coming
forward and halve the time. To halve and to hold . . . to have your
cake . . . and yours such a rich home-made. Was Sara Lee a gypsy?

My calendar is tucked in a fright in the corner of intricate plastic
lace. It's offish white. The Last Supper of 2000. Pale lilac wall weeps
through its lacy pores. Christ. He holds a heart shaped cob against
his breast. The positioning is just so. Under the matching lilac-shaded
standard lamp the room's a tip with shadow. Lopsided. All the apos-
tles are men.
Getha

(Subject: Various Sirens. Choppers)

Urban suburban and every damn half rhyme. T'night's'like soundtrack to climaxing film of Vietnam. Choppers joy riding galore. Chasing kids. Not a meek mewling lamb in sight. Dirty maelstrom low throat laugh. Multidirectional mono. Mean. I mean I feel so Friday night the furniture just sweats perfume, booze and half remembered sex. Oodle, canoodle me home a lone rangeress with untouched skin and sober as a barristocrat. Farmer-Farmer may we cross your golden river to take our father's dinner . . . look forward to seeing you big
                    bad outside world
meets faux-mad Arcadia Must dash —
Getha

(Subject: Stone Laugh)

I toy with words and twist the twisty bits of my hair 'exhibits in an inhibition' this almost sentence reoccurs without warning. What does does mean? A priceless pot on a shy rickety table. I stick my life out. I'll play divertimentos and make maps of the face of my cheeky-chops bare-breasted goddess. Such laughingly love at first sight should not go uncharted. The moment in the mind fleshed out. Hiding from seek — in the eye-level sun — in the blazing embarrassment — in the face of the back of the church — in the village — in the graveyard — in the strange little county called Rutland.

Now I'm not too sure all the apostles are men. One seems too beardless and fine jawed.

Farmer Dark-Force may we par take our father's boiled dinner as it is in heaven?

This is an ever and its lasting.
Getha.

(Subject: Falling Outs)

The blind even quivered at the iddy girl tungsten thin and burning bright fell out with all gods in a big way such as only youngage can with starry id. They conjured miniature animals for warfare but they readily scorched and rebelled.

The lambs a-lit.
                    Its face turned a shiny teaspoon to the
                          west beam that was.
Always always,
Getha.

(Subject: Breakers)

All at sea in the city.
This ash I wandered streets and turned at every café bar. Flew flew flew. My shoulders creaked with monkey and the blustery and my guardian angel a-beating my head hair to a tarnished knot. Puzzle snarled. I felt in my pocket for my tissue and pricked my finger on a cocktail stick shaped like a sword for sticky of cherries. Intending to strike at the heart of torment I picked out a lovers lock and a chunk of Irish Sea. My first concerto is in the making. It has no spots. It may yet be amphibian.

May it cross your golden river? Dark-Force Fisherman.
Getha

(Subject: Rogue Rage)

All the apostles are men but one is without a beard and leaning too willowy to Christ. Is this a trick of plastic lace? A sleight of oversight? He looks on close a she. Joan of Arc jumping icon banks, sabotaging sacred narratives. The last immovable tableau. Fire I fear will follow.
I fear also I note by night my sentences ring oddly and raw and now the day draws as I do . . . all in . . . I will cease to speak as I don't want to startle the birds from sleep. Where *do* birds sleep?
Getha

(Subject: Radio. Gales. Floods.)

What's that you say. Another great escape . . . life's an eternal
fencing match . . . keep inoutin . . . shake ma ma nature an all that
jazz . . . hips in the offing. Can Aliens make the breakthrough?
My day after day is backgrounded with radio-pulp. Flat above is
endless Jungle. What a jiggersaw. What is a jiggersaw? As yet no
flood or trickle of luck with work . . . check ads and sads and sod em
all maybe I'll robabank and Bonnie it without Clyde across the
world. Farmer-Farmer. The apostle is suspiciously perfumed.
Joan of Arc in on hold.
Getha.

(Subject: Discovery)

I'm faxing a map of Jupiter. I'm worried about the hot spot. The
new flash points are now called 'reports' as a soothing strategy for
public panic. But study the map if you please. The red seems sulky.
Not quite how red should act. My friend is close but colour blind.
He cannot throw light. He eats green strawberries. Purple doesn't
exist. He weeps for wimberries all through the season. To him the
red spot's a kiwi. I think he's obsessed with fruit. Maybe he's right.
Maybe strawberries glow with envy. Traffic lights make him hungry
not angry. But tell me about the hot spot. Is it out of sorts. May we
cross its golden river. Our father's dinner is
growing cold.
Be cool Be.
Getha.

(Subject: Amber Alert)

Hell-p!
And as I write a stranger is flickering under the leaning street-lamp.
Out the window. I wish he would choose another. This afternoon an
unseasonable heaviness of air. The city restless with shifting signs.
Rubbing undercurrents. Jumping lights. Pedestrians stage-diving
pelicans. Jaywalkers. Ill-mannered starlings. A subdued iridescence
on the necks of lame pigeons. Discoloured glister of penniless
window-shoppers. Oldsters cheesed.
A daylight moon thoroughly fed-up all round.
I wish he would go.
The flickering man.
Write soon
Getha

(Subject: Din. Neuralgic Ringings)

Did you reply? Computer curdled then crashed to obliv. Living here
is neither here. Things closing in and amazing facts curl up their
toes. I lean out the window crooning. All whole roads are up.
Diversions to nowhere everywhere. Heads ache with pneumatic
drills. When they found the frozen mammoth it still had buttercups
in its mouth. Still edible. Floral steaks. It's a time thing. All day
industrial rock . . . all powered by . . . tax . . . my notwork neuralgia
. . . dust bowls of thinks . . . are Oman and Yemen female landscape
. . . curvy dunes sucked dry . . . strangled gardens . . . Babylon . . .
pollution . . . the Americans have just bought God.
Pandemonium is the word of the day. Let us pray.
P   A   N   D   E   M   O   N   I   U   M   A   M   E   N

Getha

(Subject: Sodden)

Walls grin wetly. And H E'S there again.
Up to his knees.
        Newspaper in hand under
            the sodium ghastly.
The apostle is moving.
Do I
not that
like
Get . . .

(Subject: Back on Track)

Farmer-Farmer home safe and trying to catch straggling sheep
bleats as they galumph through the whorls of my ears: this sentence
is too long. Don't sheep ever sleep? Eep eyp eyarp. With eyes to
slice a primordial onion. To lie-side-down is-to-die. A crying shame.
Your silhouette on the hill is not a national treasure. Our nation
is shrinking and violent. Your golden river. My father's dinner.
The mill.
Last night this early morn I drove the city streets — so muggy for so
early spring. Drainy glottal stop . . . the window wide after midnight
. . . an amazed mouth . . . conversations, contretemps tittle-tat hit
earshot.

what the | out 'n' out | .crude.i cry | finglan' no
stop. . | side eer | in allin...yer | ingland
y(w)hoo. | flame in in | mind.ful...t | blonde.blui
where did . | in..anas I | throated | d.slost de
over her e.. | ..woz ...wot | ...a'll | key ...smol
yam sick | yucol me | throttle...piz | world big
(Ooh | ...leave! it a | za...ever let | cit.catrut
never)...wat | sed leave it | me hear | sit e smelt
ch | a lone bol | here you say | swerds.....m
it.babe. . . s/ | irks lukad | eat or met | ewl shut out
f/luck its | isthad'the | al bar none | shout and
bottlemate | moonooerr | ...injure...n | god alof.
. . . s/da(f)t | ..don't.be | ...jalfazi... | United. Un.
bas-t-ar | crule cry | oys ....'zchoo |
tara see u | | from |

I was cruising for cool. Foxy hot footing towards the main shop-mall. Disquieting shiver of breaking glass breaking as ever somewhere else. I drove through the heart and out the other side. Vanished. Abracadab. Walls grew massive. Stone bruising stone. Skyblotters. Humourless Victorian monoliths. Industry work-ships swaying dirty breath down neck. Bones against ghosts. Ran through umbilical bridges and archways. Past scrambled. Crashed into newness. Lean reflecting glass. Imported steel. Bouncing light. Loveliness.

I headed home into I.

The apostle sashayed round the last supper à la Rita Hayworth à la laa Gilda. My heart jumped in my mouth with respect. Window boxes grew miniature Edens. The sun some moment will stream. Break into fox-trot round table legs. My heart feels like a host. It sticks to my roof. I take it out and put it about. Leavened wild life everywhere. Gone-to-earth goes up the cry. I need late-night biscuits with salt. Come see me in my urban heaven. Meet flying rats and flagrant saints.

It is quiet now. The apostle is still. Sweet city catnaps before sunrise. Air cleaner and chill fresh. I watch News 24. The Americans have just bought Dawn. Stars beyond the streetlights. I lean out my window to croon. Yes, there he is. An unearthly hour. Ginger shock, lamp-leaning, under the manufractured moon.
G.

Faustus: A Travesty

Faustus began to practise scales
little divilish
arty dodger conjured imps
whirly dervish
meet the morrow.

A conference with Mephisto and his cronies
as the morning snuggles by-the-sea.
A parley a parley we need a
third parley.
Conclusion. Occlusion.

Jeremy Paxman: Cumon cumon cumon!
Dr Faustus: What was the question. Again?

Faustus set his blood in a saucer
on a warm ash
and a wit what followeth
came writing.

What manners appeared
his sights he shewed hem
how cause kept a xopy
just for effect.

To win to win proceeded his
damnable life of militant
service to lip Mephisto.

Unto his spirit Mephisto dreamed
a dream that Faustus saw hell in his seep
of sleep he inserted the dream
and questioned.

Jeremy Paxman: So what's going on Dr Faustus?
Dr Faustus: It's not that simple Jeremy.

With spirits of matters
what is the?
Hell concerned put forth realms
and Lucifer's sorrow fell afterwards.

Disputation betwixt Faustus
and Spirit. To know the secrets
and pains of whether damned-devils
might grace and favour or if a loss is in the offing.
A game of big dice. A toss beyond.

*Jeremy Paxman: But you can't seriously
believe that?
Dr Faustus: But of course I don't believe that.
You're not listening to what I say Jeremy.*

Faustus fell into despair.
Himself having put forth
a quest then him and him
fell at variance.
A whole lot of falling going on.

Whereupon the whole rout of
divels appeared threatening him
sharply with weapons of nerves
holding analgesics behind their
hairy backs.

Faustus was carried through the air
to heavens bent and saw how the
sky and planets ruled he wrote
one letter to his friend.

*Jeremy Paxman: But you say in your letter quite clearly
Dr Fau . . .
Dr Faustus: Excuse me for interrupting but a letter is
a private nothing and you know it . . .*

Faustus went around the world
in eight days and in his went he had
a sight of Paradise. And Palestine. Sierra
Leone. Belgrade. Baghdad. Nuremberg.
The Home Counties.

And a certain comet peered in
and flicked its tail. He desired to know
and know it all now
the meaning thereof that vex men
to fall in thunder.

*Jeremy Paxman: We're talking about destabilising
world markets.*
*Dr Faustus: No we're talking a comet can crash to earth.
Don't you see. We need nuclear weapons and quick. And sand.
And big bags.*
Jeremy Paxman: You're losing it aren't you?

The Emperor requested to see
his cunning. The women his lingus.
Hart's horns and a knight's head slept
themselves into sweet revenge.

Fair Helen. Ah so fair. Almost red-haired
in her beauty. And on a Sunday. Wheels
clatter from the bedecked wagon and
four jugglers cut the others' head offa
for the ultimate juggle act.

*Jeremy Paxman: Let me put it this way Dr Faustus
don't you think you're getting a bit fanciful?*
Dr Faustus: Oh come off it Jeremy.

Great powers spawn great sillies:
Serving students to a blinding
stop he opens mouths of
drunken clowns.
Plays merry jests in courts
with castles on feasts
for measure shocks a bishop
in his wine cellar.

A great army in his extremity
would have injured his journey
so Mephisto brought seven of his
fairest women. Hips spanning eternity —
reinforced gussets.

Jeremy Paxman: You said certain drunken Dutchmen
were abused by their own conceit and self-imagination.
Are you sure about that?
Dr Faustus: You're twisting my words.

Faustus deceived them all.
With his won blood
he made a marriage of sorts
and shewed strange sights
in his nineteenth on ninetieth year gathered:
a mass of money consumed his life.

Stand still ye everlasting spheres.
Tragedy is in the Air.
A thousand people of Wittenberg
engendered me . . . weeps Faustus
in his conjured beer with but one
last hour of drinking time.

To die so miserabilis as the clock
strikes brunch. Faustus clucks 'Come not
Mephistopheles I'll burn my books'

Jeremy Paxman: Dr Faustus. Are you up to the job?
Dr Faustus: Of course I am Jeremy.

The second mocking the third
mocking the fourth
mocking the
past is the future.

Jeremy Paxman: You haven't answered my question.
Dr Faustus: Because I am the answer. There is no need
to look at tomorrow's papers Jeremy.

FLUVIUM

Fluvium

(espial)

Abandoned moon buggies.
Fly-blown.
Will soon be cold.
As cod.
Is.

Breathe fey cloud.
Wreathe ectoplasm.
Seethe.
It.

Drifting cells.
Interior war.
All out creation cluster.
The city has reached it.
Weakend.
Fluvium.

Inaudible closure of love.
Slowmo blink.
Lash-lash.
Heart-fakers.

Breathe fey cloud.
Wreathe ectoplasm.
Seethe
IT
wreath
it
like

(listeners)

Ina dark-dark
her little.
Ina dark-dark
so little.
*Rappa rappa
rappa rappa
u'most a caress.*

*Rappa rappa
rappa rappa*
AYE....

'er blueberry hair
UpendS

two lips at moonlit-late
viridian neon
lit two lips
at door lit-late
viridian
neon at
door lip
lit-late

Ina dark-dark
her little.
Ina dark-dark
so little.
Rappa rappa
rappa rappa
AYE.......
'er blueberry hair
UpendS

*Rappa rappa
R*ue-rue.......
Is there anybody there?
(Is there anybody there?)
Said . . .

(very ´very)

It was a *very very very*
curled up
beer mat.
Singular. Stiff.
It
r~o~c~k~k~k~kt
a~n~d
r~o~c~k~k~k~kt

time dripped unnoticed
~and~then~
~and~then~
it stopt.
Blotted out
and wotted
not what to do ~
transmogrified.

>   *(wayafter aching midnight)*

Night of urban freefall
funlovers.
Muted creams
dressing and gunfire
.O-loud.
The song's **a-dumb.**

Uncomic a arrow h h arrow
h ar hrow
H A R R O W.
Uncomic harrow.
Puftup faces.
Snake root
noxious **tox**
taxes
fixes
capillaries of fish
spittle
death and what not.
Take any shape but *THAT.*

(floresce)

Loonshine~on~loverskins~
drifting~cells~spangle~ab~

(A flutter and slump of leaves.
To the floor the book had flew
and out fell the condemned sentence)

I
I went
I went looking (at night)
I went looking at night (between swinging doors)
I went looking at night between swinging doors (for my drunken)
I went looking at night between swinging doors for my drunken
(stage May Queen) father

(wayafter aching midnight)

slike . . .

light?

slike . . .

slike eye-light
slike
eyelights of
animal
in headlight
in night feast
in bright cast
in fast feel
in heat

oh how they
fix-you
witch-you
wayafter
WAYAFTER
WAYAFTER

(a............m............)

(ghast)

They closed the shocker.
The paranoid knock. *Node.*
Colourless noise.
Electro-bacterial dis
ease . . . .
seeping rich
stealth
con
tamin-a-tion
(shone)

Dart the light-lack room.
Dart the light-back
        death moths
daft and after us
be-by
        gone
ar-tificial
            day
made claggy
dreamery
        flicker
germ pods
parti...c...parti..c
exits skid

at breakneck
reel the roosh
it came
O
pen **M**
    Outhed

Yip!
Eerie
question scar-scary
whaaaaaaaaaaat
Whichever way yis eyes.
Whichever way yis eyes
wwww**w**atter.

(metablethers)

Lid em! Label!
Preserve the rare
the roar the
prim wild
rose rare
wild roar
rise

The daisy is not for turning.

Blebshed.
      Shudded.   Malkingrim.
         Axhy.

      Mal-shed.   Blebshed.   **Shudded.**
      Malkingrim.   *Headaxhy.*

Fly chinchilla!

YamI YamO	leather shed
grin grow	feather bled
rushes	shouldered
O	sweet songing
sweet	rare roar
O	rose grows
sorry	prim rise
O	sing while
dew	sing while

sing while
'er blueberry hair
stalagmites

(fusile)

crackabunch-o-knuckle
joints
skeletal
arpeggio.

Brood.
Hood.
Snakebit in
drinkstain
grin-glow
in
carpet
in
wintry

we'll awe go far.
Far too far too.

This mornings light is
still
tonight unslept
some laugh

come-come to me soothing
sleep
and soothe my weep
in
loveliness

(wayafter aching midnight)

THREE
SHORT SORTIES

Epicentre

Darkness hit Paris flat at the flick of a switch. She drew a blind across a lycanthropic moon. Suggestively detectable. A hu-manish shape adjusts its ears. A stab in the dark goes wildly off-course. Bad direction. B Movie. Falters. Stumbles. Makes way down close and dreaky East End alley. Cat rubbing up against her leg. Persian carpets. By design. Darkness is a kind kind of relief. Mercy-mother-ma. It has been a longlong day. Not a glitch of air. A bauble. Passionless evening of weepable proportions. Month-upon-month of Sundays. Without camber. Tangents. Not a hint of a half of a turned up ha laugh. He clicks on the gas tap. The single gold ring on his bony finger twists. Catches light. She strikes the match. It splits. Rotten. Slightly burning back hand. His hand shakes. To hold the spoon steady needs a carafe of soothings. To hold anything. A sequence of moments. A sequin. Broad spectrum miracle needed. Strong-eyed medicine. Mega-magic.

She strikes again. Cat flinch. Got it. Light closes her eyes. The dark rings. Olivenite. Walnut. Pure black pure silk. Skin. Stockings. Dashes of synthetic perfection. Cut-glass bowls of fresh. Blossoms. Semen smells. Peachiwhite magnolia. Her skin is. His skin. There it goes. G-god. As clockwork. His tock-tock arm jerks. Spills. Just a bit. Gist a liddle bit. Spills one or two or drib more grains. But always. It's the but what bugs. Buries under skin. Lodges tic hard. A windblown of easy grains. Silly bloody specks of almost nothing. Why such upset. He sighs. Word weary. World sigh. The high point of a pointless. Frowst. She smoothes her skirt. Marmish. Fatale. Nicotine coloured rings. Eyes blear soft-edged in candle flame. She rests her hands catastrophically on her thighs. A flying boat enters the vision. Odds on an air raid. Nerves stir. Flinch. Cat's back. Blinding guilt everywhere. Mirrors. Plush stuff. Overbearing perfume. Sniff the lair. A finger and thumb snap beat. Somewhere. Tonight's the night. Converging of epicentres.

Pick-up money. Hand-over. Pass-it on. Paid-for pash on delivery. Tag. Frameshift. Daytodayto. How futile can—can—it get. She lifts her arm. Tonight her elsewhere heart is not in-it. When is it ever. Detritus of devotion. Over. Done. Fat-bottomed businessmen. Unheavenly satellites. Freak-faced moons. Crooning gaseous noises. Hellish pastyfaced lunarscapes. He turns his face towards the outer wall. Grilled. Heavy metal stripes. Footsteps drag a shadow past. Cast. Her arm comes down hard on futility. The jaunty flick of the wrist. Mist not missed. It has the desired effect. Mewl. She turns her head to the outer wall. Why? Footsteps reverse. Why? What mimics who? Odds on. An air rake. Glidership. Skeletal. A cockney voice scythes through the grating. Cursing. And another. And another. Exclusively male. Far out loud. Practised deep. Crake. They go. Crake. Her name.

She thinks she hears her name. As it happens it happens. From time to time. Hears her dead mother call. Tease ready! Suddenly so hot. Liquor. All in. He spikes. The brew is brewed. Daydone. Blast the grains. Forgeddum. The circle of white liquid mesmerizes. She stares into the flame. Sounds from the river drift. Bounce. Reflect off windows. Fall back into the Seine. Tonight. Is the night. The light cuts through her eyelids. A welt. A face. Tired. Globes. He sighs. Paced anger. She draws a blind. Across. A cross. To bare. Her face she turns to face her moon face turns towards the outer wall. He yelps. With really-feely. Pouring floorwards down his bod. Scaldy. Weak light clams to her retina. Imprints. Red and guilt. He flinches. In the midst of her vision. She hears her name. Parawordy. Partitioned. In the midst of an explosive sound. He grips his heart. Grips wherever it is he thinks his heart should be. Grips his pain as the cat rubs against her other. Leg. She emits a low-slow animal moan. Omens from somewhere near the Thames. Docklands. An almighty shattering. Glass. Her heart has fled. And crockery. She turns towards. The flying boat. The grill. Slain glass occlusions. Aflame. Her name she hears. Way down. The bottle breaks. He stiffens. Guides his feet. Through grains. Shards. Constellations. Dripping masonry. Alike ghosts. Dayafter. Aftermath. Uneasy daylight. Burnt milk. Boiled. Spilt. No cry.
N-no. Instant bitter-tongued coffee stains.

Figurehead

How'st her name written bove bed? Not as in hospital. Felt-tipped transience. This is bedsit. Dampland. Faint gas smells. Couple of blots cross top of washbasin. Damphappy slaters rim-around cracked porcelain. Scummy. Sicky stuff edging the precipice. Woodlice. S'crunchy. He'd said. Like biscuits. Also. He added smirkyling. They are cousins to shrimps. Her fork hesitated. Pink-juiced trinklets. Sulky lips. Sudden pout o shrimps. Hated biscuits. Crunchy things. How he'd smirked. How? Don't ask. How? Well smuglike. 'Ismug. Mouth full of crumbs and crustaceans. Lips purplish. Thin as. As. As. As. As. How thin? Lips as thin as water. As. Water. Tap water. Thin as a drip. God how she 'ated shrimps. God. Good-not.

The duvet slithered tut floor. Slithered down to-take-away crumbs. Squashed fag butts. Cover garish. Fur kids. American cartoons. Bright beyond. Beyond what? What? What? Dunno. Bright beyond reason. Necessity. The sun. It absorbed food stains. Drink stains. Sex stains. Smelt faintly off-gas. Sugar. Exclamation! Sweat. As the curtains are closed it is more muted than usual. A blessing. A blessing amongst curses. Many curses.

The letters of her name run. Her name runs. It has been painted in a paint. Above her bed. On peeling wallpaper. In raw sienna. Raw runny name. Bunny. No. No. No. Of course its not Bunny. Seemed a nice idea. Ivy. No. No. Not Ivy either. Neat. Ivy crept down wall. The tendril of letters entwined. Twisted. Dripped. O. So. But no. The letters were creepy. Positioned with insane obliteration. Loop spiralling into her left ear. On her side. Against. A spike of hair needles a spike of paint dripped down from the I. Caked mascara. Deep frosted eye shadow. Flaking. Whitish sheet. Half on. Half sidled. Slipped between her legs. She rides it like a sky-witch rides a-brooom. Cut. Cross her body. One leg. One buttock. One breast and brown nipple. One arm. One angular unkissable shoulder. One scuffed scabbed knee. One freezing cold foot fish skin glowing in the semi-dark. There is a angry bruise on her upper arm.

That's right. A angry. A angry. Skeins of cheap rolled gold chain hanging. Hung from her neck. Wrists. Cheap and thin. Thin beyond. Beyond? Beyond? Dunno. Thin beyond something beyond the stars. Novas. Super models. Beyond belief. Beyond blethers. Transparent Ones. Light seeping through her body. More than. Luminosity glimmers from within. Face fierce with ruined energy. Ship figure head. Goldish. Cold colours of hydro-suffocation. Marine green. Blue. Blood-brown. Brown-brown. Occult blood weeds. Vicious red pout. Thread veined blisted glass. Thick painted eyebrows loggered. Knotted wrack. Scrolled aggression. Eyes chiselled to kill diabolic monster from the deep. Gouge. Gouge. This is enough. Godnot. I cannot read it.

And opposite. Opposite her lying behind bottle green velveteen dream and net curtains breaths. Yes-eyes open. Yes-eyes? Yes. Yes-eyes. Open on direction of closed door. Unblinking. He stands with back to wall. Has stood hours. Spooklooking up at window. Her. There is a bruise on his upper arm. His lips thin. Dripping tap water.

From a window opposite a woman stares at him staring up at the window. For hours. And now a point in those hours. The critical now point. Someone. Who? Who? I cannot see. Make them out. Great clouds of some stuff. Some? Obscuring. I cannot see clearly. I wish I could. Someone I cannot see clearly comes a cracking open. Asunder. Cram. Knuckles of the meanest. Peeved and buckling all silences of the room. A knock to quake the troubled soul. Incite hurricanes across the globe. Globe eyes pinned on opening door.

Unblinking.

The woman sees something. Bad. Something bad is wriggling. Wriggling out the corner of his mouth. Something wriggles out. She turns to tell her dead husband. Tells as a late bus passes with a shriek. Light blocked out for a split. Spine jerk. Tells him everything. Sometimes yells. Has to. Yells out of this world. See. See. See. He stares at the window. She stares at him.

Eyes pinned hard. Skewered. Beyond. The doorway. Clouding up. Shortly the circuit will blow. Cleaving silences. The room becomes shattered. She doubles up and yells. SEE! In the wake of such commotion a kind of wriggling is beginning. Beginning to take place. Heart mummers. Unearth tremors. Infinitesimal vibrations. Beneath the bed eleven embalmed sparrows commence to shake in their feather pierced skins.

Kiss

Tricker. Very. Trapt. Very. Deep. Tarmac. Swelt. Each white-socked foot sink. In. Upover ankles. S'will. Managing to pull. Out. Just. Swill. Just juicy slops for them starving. Sinkers. Absence of. Of resistance setsoff. Panicky. Teeth edges. A sickening lack of solidity. Jellied legs. Boned. Hard urban pathways turn treack. Slurry. Black-black. Holding weight. Cloy of comfort. If she looses blackness she loses. O-all. Watcha death. Watch. If she can just make. Make it. Watch that spot. That. That street end. If she can just. Just. Whaddaday.

As she turns her head her vision skids. Joy driven. A car swerves to a void a. Cat. Misses void. Blown up crisp bag. One-minute-cat-head. Next. Both go pop. Deflate to same re. Sound. P.O.P. Crisp bag red white blue. Cat head red black blue. Almost united colours. Almost united taste. Fish flavoured. Low fat. Salty.

Joydriven thirteen year old before time behind wheel careers madly. More madly after come urban hunters. Just following procedures. Unleashing demons. Leech. Night-night blue enamelled insects swarm. Streets. Skies. Infect with seepings. She heaves. Ho. She'll never do it. She gets no further each second. What's wrong. As crazed hunters pass they pierce her ears. Branded with screech and siren. Chopper din. Nostrils seared with burnt rubber. For this she is truly thankful. Sear and din. A qualitative pain. Solid. Tangible. Unpavements. A contrast too poignant. She holds back a sob. A. Arrow of. Courses through. Her. Inside arms. Down inside arms. Centres palms. Fingerclicks across chest. Fans out into facial nerves and upwards into darkend chicaneries of her brain. Eventually it will stain her entire. But for now. Deep. Deep downside.

Vertigo. Knocks her for six. Knocks her right off. She momentarily catches end of street. Funny. Yellowbricked terraced houses. Inexplicably erotic. Behind. Pure slabs of high rise. Roof tops rock against sky. S'feels all at sea. Sick. Swell. Not swell. Eccetera. In quick succession. Ariel antennae lose reception. Irrational bugs pick up diseased droppings. Overflow of paranoid interference. Rash insects covering what seems every centimetre. Frantic scratch and itch of legs. Still running. Still. Innermost unseemly fashion. She is. She is coming down to meet them. She. What will she do. A body with no longer a head is a puzzle to comfort. What can one. Sey? What do farmers. Sey? Hey headless chicken! Be still your soul. Stay it. Still. Probably not. She will say nothing. Will stroke its legs. Stickly gig. g.le. No. A. She will watch with imaginary mothers. Watch it. She is falling headlong. Joy. Steering. Cut sharp. Aching high. He. Outrageously beautiful for one so young. Reaching his corner. Hunters reaching theirs. She hitting ground. Hitting momentary distraction. Sickening impact. Oh it is sickening. It makes a deep set impression. If she can just. Just. If she can. Stomach this. Stomach street corner. Undergoing progress. Undergoing ongoing. Goings. Very on. Hunters. Boy.

Well we have all seen collisions. This one. Well. Hunters well strapped. Padded. Visored. Boy. Well not. Very much not. He journeys through two windscreens. An orgasmic trajectory. Kisses hunter. Yes. Just one. Though. It is a kiss to death. Twice. It passes everything. Two sets of teeth. Enmeshed. Defying division. Rest. You. You can imagine for yourselves. I cannot. I cannot make it out. She picks herself off pavement. Glance. Glances at legs. Wipes away. Wipes. With her sweatshirt sleeve. With the heart on her sweatshirt sleeve. Now. Her legs are running. She can just make it. Just. Running. Red heart running. West. Ever west. Setting. Sea somewhere. Now. Sea turn on. Sea and so too traffic lights. And so too. And no that poem did not contain even one blood word. 'Twas merely written on red paper.

NINE

LITTLE ONES

The Sad Lions of Seville

Downwind the Alcazar
up the reeky fish.
They are so miffed a
foursome prowling static
in their alone stretch
of facial droop
to the point of
rich.

Who counts the small
hours but the
weary
the
sick
and these
sad lions of
Seville

pulling such funnies
upon your life
had nothing so gaunt
upon it
to stare.

Bulls happier by far
in their bored to fattened
death
than these lions in their
none and
briefly glorified
telling.

So who shot Lorca up the arse
down the road?
Not we say the lions
with our hearts clamped in irons.
No, not you by glimmers
but you
you little cocky sparrows
with pois'nd arrows and
a gun.

Inanimate Moves

Wine glasses explod-
dead
en masse
ex-
static sylla-
bubs o
what can the
matter be
under
arty-
fishy sun
psycho-tic
gesturals
pan-
ache
on a panic-picnic.

Of which witch-
likely
tendencies
is this display
in aid of?
What goes on
in the where of
your minds ?

(Our)
fleshyfriends
withywords
'yes' and 'I'
gone missing
a withered
beat
at
(Your)
spectacular
ocular
I'mmolation.

*   *   *

It wasn't that
the book placed
just so
was not actually
placed
just so
as the cynical
bent in its
pegged back
lips
that send us skidding

*   *   *

The champers
cork flew with a force
twelve good
bods and
true
could not have
reasonably
doubted the
impossible
trajectory beyond
the
bathroom's
new blue
shadow-shock

*   *   *

It takes a robust mind
to keep inanimates in place.

They slake their thirst
on the spaces between
angelical membranes
and unmapped
geographies of
spirit.

Autofluence

'Smudging is 'n ancient car-craft
           used by trad-Amer-Indians'

Unwanted spirit hitch-hikers?
Smudge 'em!
      Exorcise a fit of the *bads:*

grab herbs
sage, burnt cedar
smudge sticks
light blow
smoulder
catch
hot ash
ina fireproof
gently
waft
to the
      four corners
of the
      auto
      da fé

Found Confab in Fanelli's
(New York 1997)

'How's . . . ?'
Oh him. Fraid he wos keeld in L.A.'
'. . . . .'

'Drug pushi . . .'
'. . . . .'

'Piddy. Niis guy'
'. . . . .'

'Tomado sauce . . .'
'. . . . .'

'Thaysay id's good for cancer'
'No kiddin! Tomado sauce?'

Avoiding Other People's Accidents
(England 2000)

And so it came to pass:
travelling the London
Orbital
at the speed of butter
fingers
unwrapping
cling
filmed
damp sandwiches

Indwelling
intercoastal nerve blocks
                              accumulation ov fluids
terminal
r
       e s
               t
l   es s
  n
       e   ss

If you want to go-
get out your-
mind-
that-
gap-
-

Found Church Guide

'At the west end of the tower stands Sheela Nargigs [sic] a Celtic
fertility goddess. In Christian times her hideous [sic] features put
the devil to flight. These figures are generally seen in Ireland and
there is no good reason for her to be in Braunston. [my italics]
She was found face downwards as a doorstep.'

Response

There is no good reason
for anything but a
beaming English face
we should
not pin on the Irish.

Her glappy lips span worlds
warming cockles to guffaw away
the damned devil
odd perky breasts
set flagrant terror alight
with fertility guff
an' fibs as stiff as *treacle*
'sif naked
woman couldn't laugh
an let it all hang out baht
want o sprogs — bah!

Consigned to be trammelled
under clothed Xian hooves
not worth the earth
dug 'n' dug upright
lo and be-bold!

(No. Stuft away proper from
full frontal lobe)

There she squat
up — carrying-on
lewdly hidden
behind a sniggering wall of wall.

Unhappy Heaven

'There is no surer way of keeping possession than by devastation'
                                                                    Machiavelli

hear hearts x at a slant   italicized
clandest   movering-angels
cruise
like all as at sea   (soulslost glib the fishers)
hover
as on freeways   (drivers sign it mirage)
wing mirrors sprout
                    sore
fingers thrum
to quick dimin all knowns nnnn
retro in-a-flut   (the fleet mo-mo)

Here's not a rainy night in Soho 's more
a sprink of damp gravity with a dash
of crusht
iced mirrors in a suchness   (designated)
celestial corners   *   *   *
                              *
                    *   *   *

panelled-words warm
smoke-dyed glass as
golden as . . . at-night-bulbs
tethering together two weeny
animals falling hopelessly in
The French House squashy with
lovers and other English refugees

Sacred (or scared) little voices
chunner on the verge of
profane arias. out-broke.

'*Nervous euphoria*' *she thunderacks*
from the froggish undergrowth
(pond life indeed us becomes)
sacred (or scared) (or scarred)
the humours of the *devastated* are-ra rare *order*

heaven the absence of hell
heaven misheard of an ending

melancholy Dürer do-id again
doodle and fix this
bile in copper plated myth.

Fetch another frosted glass
clenched
and bitter teeth snap and spit
the vitreous rim
a waning-half moon
pink und
piled in yittle heaps
of transitory bliss...t

The Physical Letters

eye-spy   mole-blink   un-earth
orbicular
message of displaced image
elliptic
jerking upright fires
lanceolate
light-eyes
rhomboidal
stored moment in a centre
cordate
direct hit refraction
sagittate
demarcating non-terrestrial territories
spinose
radial-eyes towards outer-zones
flabellate
craziest life-swim
undulate
neon-whorled-world

The Incorruptible Pilgrimage

*We pilgrimage
to Rue de Bac*

Scouring bright Paris
for shades
& St Catherine Laboure's
Incorruptible Body
we consulted the
well-stuffed horse
to be kicked forthright
up the Rue
Taxidermical
comforting our Rue
de Bac.

*Entering the
enshrined
entrance
d*

In the chapel of
doll-kitsch glitter
'pink is
the navy-blue of
India' is
an understatement
working on the wrong
continent in the wrong
country in
the city of
infallible
gargoyles.

*Going through
the motions*

Kow-bowing an oddsome
genuflect
the transaction subsumed
impostors
naked and marred
without rosary beads—
guilt-inspired bouquets.

We suck the sugar
coated corpse
encased in
glass

> And there the body lies
> and there lies the body
> and who believes the
> seeing of
> sees the hallowed
> stepping on our hearts.

glass

> She-afterlyfe a
> hairball unravel at root &
> flourish from a vivid.
> She-nails grow apace
> in a state of immaculate manicure
> poised for the rodent-toed clicker
> clicker across 'lectronic keyboards.
> Percussioned mockeries
> claw back favours for
> she-is the Impress of
> dun-coloured
> kingdom
> come graftingly
> dull.

Great graces
granted

> Protected from dynamic
> harm by neck-hanging a
> miraculous medallion
> (purchased with
> loose centimes)
> Lo! Stewing in its blue lagoon
> eleven shooting stars—
> the constellation of the
> European Union.

Notes and Acknowledgements

The Transparent Ones was originally the performance work *Metablethers of Getha* and was first performed at Brighton College of Art. The final section *The Unspeakable Softness of Flesh* first appeared in West Coast Line and Poetry Wales in radically altered forms. This work is in memory of and in thanks to all the patients I worked with over a period of six and a half years as Creative Writer in a hospice and in particular to the memory of my dear friend Tony who happily lived too long to be included in this series but unhappily not long enough to see this book in print.

Trilogy was originally published as a Gargoyle edition.

Songings was written in collaboration with the musician Martin Archer. It's available on CD from Voiceprint under the title *Angel High Wires*.

Dream Drover was originally published by Gratton Street Irregulars.

Hidden Cities was commissioned by The Ruskin School of Fine Art, Oxford University, as part of a series of 'alternative' bus tours around 5 English Cities. Each invited artist/writer was allocated a city. A shortened recorded version of the tour first appeared on an *Audio Arts Magazine* cassette.

Manufractured Moon was originally commissioned as a radio drama.

Faustus: A Travesty. For readers outside the U.K., Jeremy Paxman is a presenter and interviewer of the late night news programme Newsnight and is notorious for his aggressive and brusque interviewing technique.

Fluvium was first performed as a collaboration between Monk & Archer at The Grapes in Sheffield. It is now available on CD from Discus records.

The Physical Letters was commissioned for an exhibition of that name by the artist Tom Hackett. The poem first appeared in an encrypted form on a 'tombstone' in the The Angel Row Gallery in Nottingham. It was first printed in English under the title *In Between The Leaves* in *The Paper*.

Texts in this book have also appeared either in their original forms or variations in the following anthologies and magazines:

The Gig, Oasis, Terrible Work, Other, Pharos, Gare du Nord, SVP, Boxkite, Nedge, Raddle Moon

Thank you for flying through the thunder